HOW TO
KNIT

HOW TO
KNIT

TECHNIQUES AND PROJECTS
FOR THE COMPLETE BEGINNER

TINA BARRETT

THE GUILD OF MASTER CRAFTSMAN

PUBLICATIONS

First published 2013 by
Guild of Master Craftsman Publications Ltd
Castle Place, 166 High Street, Lewes,
East Sussex BN7 1XU

Reprinted 2014

ISBN 978 1 86108 916 8

PUBLISHER Jonathan Bailey
PRODUCTION MANAGER Jim Bulley
MANAGING EDITOR Gerrie Purcell
SENIOR PROJECT EDITOR Dominique Page
EDITOR Cath Senker
MANAGING ART EDITOR Gilda Pacitti
ART EDITOR Rebecca Mothersole
DESIGNER Rob Janes
ILLUSTRATORS Peters & Zabransky
PHOTOGRAPHERS Sarah Cuttle & Rebecca Mothersole

Colour origination by GMC Reprographics
Printed and bound in China

CONTENTS

INTRODUCTION

My dear grandmother taught me to knit when I was only eleven years old. She was a patient soul who could knit and finish a sweater in only a few days. Naively, I believed I would just pick up the needles and my fingers would work the yarn as skilfully as she did. Alas, initially, the needles felt like live lobsters in my hand and the yarn had a will of its own. Stitches came and went – some too tight, some too loose, many dropped and laddered but then – oh joy, a perfect one and then another! Gradually, and with gritted teeth and my tongue poking out stubbornly, I found I was actually knitting. Over the years, with practice and patience, I too could whip up a sweater in only a few days.

More than that, I feel bereft without some sort of knitting project on the go. The rhythm and reward of making beautiful knitted fabric cannot be overstated. I realize how lucky I was. Gran was always on hand to help unravel mistakes, show me how to pick up stitches and sew up my knitting. But, it occurred to me: what if there was no patient relative, friend or teacher on hand?

I wrote this book with that idea in mind. Think of it like a kindly woman, guiding you through your first steps into the skill of knitting. I have tried to keep things simple and easy to follow with step-by-step illustrations to steer you through. I have avoided the 'learner's scarf' as I find it is too long and tedious

and is rarely completed. Instead, I have designed smaller, good-looking projects using good-quality yarn and embellishments to give them a luxe feel. Nothing is more important to all knitters – beginners included – than to be able to finish a project, really love it and actually wear or use it proudly.

BEFORE
YOU START

YARNS

My aim is to design small projects that a beginner can definitely finish without growing bored and frustrated. In addition, the projects have to be gorgeous so that you don't throw them in the back of a dark cupboard never to be seen again. With simple projects, the easiest way to achieve this is to use the best-quality yarn you can afford. The finished article will look luxurious and, if cared for properly, will last for many years to come.

FIBRES AND WEIGHTS

There are two main considerations when choosing a yarn: what it is made of and how thick it is. I always try to use natural fibres in my knitwear designs, such as alpaca, merino, pure wool and vegetable fibres such as soy and cotton. You will find that each type of yarn has a different feel, drape and texture – its own unique personality. Knitwear designers choose each yarn according to its purpose; for example, soft yarn such as alpaca for babies, rougher wool types such as Herdwick for outer garments, including coats and jackets, and cashmere or silk for a glamorous evening stole.

Also, yarn can be skinny or fat. As a general rule, skinny yarns require skinny knitting needles and will take longer to grow than fat yarns, which will knit up quickly with equally fat needles.

BALL BANDS

Yarn may come in a ball or a hank but will always have a ball band. This paper band is a mine of information with useful facts you will need to know when knitting with that particular yarn. Do not throw it away until you have completed the project. I have made this mistake a few times and lived to rue the day when I decided I needed another ball but had no record of the dye lot or shade number needed to order more.

DYE LOTS

When buying yarn, remember that it is always dyed in batches or lots, so always check the dye lot on the ball band carefully. Make sure that all the numbers match, otherwise there may be a colour variation when you change balls and your finished garment might turn out to be a disappointment. This is even more important when selecting yarn dyed using organic colours; the finished product can vary quite significantly from batch to batch. Make sure you order plenty of the same dye lot and ask for a 'lay-by' service if you're not sure of the amount you will need.

GUIDE TO BALL BAND INFORMATION

- Yarn name and brand

- Shade number (and sometimes shade name)

- Weight of the ball, e.g. 50g, 100g

- Yardage of wool

- What the yarn itself is made of, such as pure merino or 50% polyester and 50% pure wool

- Washing and drying instructions

- Knitting needle size recommendation

- Approximate tension when using recommended needles

YARN SUBSTITUTION

Not everyone can afford top-end yarn, and there is nothing wrong with substituting to suit your pocket. However, if you choose to substitute the yarns recommended in the pattern there are several points you will need to bear in mind:

Firstly, always choose the same weight yarn to substitute with.

Secondly, check the yardage on your preferred yarn. It will be written on the ball band (see page 13). There may be less or more per ball than on the recommended type. In this case, you will need to allow for extra or fewer balls, so take time to work it out carefully or ask for assistance.

Finally, always knit up a tension swatch (see page 23) in your substitute yarn before starting the project so you can check that the stitch sizes match and the finished item will come out the correct size.

1 *Ball of 4-ply yarn with size 2.25mm needles.*

2 *Ball of DK yarn with size 4mm needles.*

3 *Ball of Aran yarn with size 5mm needles.*

4 *Ball of chunky or super-chunky yarn with size 8mm needles.*

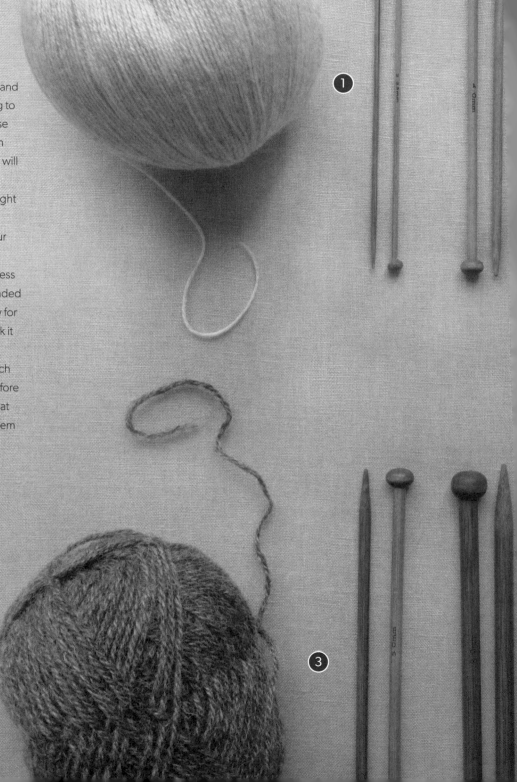

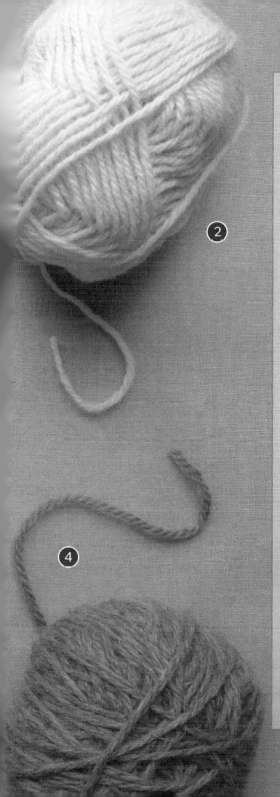

GUIDE TO YARN WEIGHT, NEEDLE SIZE AND TENSION

SIZE 1 YARN WEIGHT: SUPER FINE

UK 4-ply; US sock, fingering and baby weight

Average tension: 27–32 stitches over 4in (10cm)

Recommended needle sizes:
UK sizes 2.25–3.25mm
US sizes 1–3

SIZE 2 YARN WEIGHT: FINE

UK lightweight double knitting; US sport and baby weight

Average tension: 23–26 stitches over 4in (10cm)

Recommended needle sizes:
UK sizes 3.25–3.75mm
US sizes 3–5

SIZE 3 YARN WEIGHT: LIGHT

UK double knitting; US light worsted

Average tension: 21–24 stitches over 4in (10cm)

Recommended needle sizes:
UK sizes 3.75–4.5mm
US sizes 5–7

SIZE 4 YARN WEIGHT: MEDIUM

UK and US Aran; US worsted and Afghan

Average tension: 16–20 stitches over 4in (10cm)

Recommended needle sizes:
UK sizes 4.5–5.5mm
US sizes 7–9

SIZE 5 YARN WEIGHT: BULKY

UK chunky; US craft, rug

Average tension: 12–15 stitches over 4in (10cm)

Recommended needle sizes:
UK sizes 5.5–8mm
US sizes 9–11

SIZE 6 YARN WEIGHT: SUPER BULKY

UK super chunky/US bulky roving

Average tension: 6–11 stitches over 4in (10cm)

Recommended needle sizes:
UK sizes 8mm and larger
US size 11 and larger

BASIC TOOLS AND EQUIPMENT

You might think there are only two basic things needed for knitting: a pair of needles and some yarn. That is true, but it is helpful to have a few other little notions in your project bag too, as detailed below. Most can be picked up easily and cheaply from your local yarn store or online.

1 KNITTING NEEDLES

These are available in metal, plastic and bamboo. I favour the bamboo ones but this is purely personal. Experiment with all the different types to find the one that suits you. Choose a medium or shorter length to start with. If the needles are too long, you will find them awkward and tricky to handle initially.

Knitting needles come in a range of sizes suited for different yarn weights: skinny yarn requires skinny needles and fat yarn needs fat needles. Check the materials section at the beginning of each project to find out which size you will need to use.

Cable needles are small double-ended needles for working cables. They come in two styles: curved or straight. I prefer the curved, which have a dip in the centre for holding stitches secure when they are not being worked. Use fat cable needles when working fat yarn and skinny cable needles when working skinny yarn.

2 CALCULATOR

If you hate maths, then a calculator is indispensable for working out tension, especially if you have chosen a different yarn to the one stated on the pattern.

3 ROW COUNTER

This is not essential but handy if you are working pattern repeats or are decreasing on a set row. Just click the button at the end of every row worked to keep track of the number worked.

4 STITCH MARKERS

These are small rings, which you place on your needle between the stitches. They simply hang there and act as a reminder to increase or decrease or to mark lace repeats. You slip them off one needle and onto the other as you work along the row.

5 CROCHET HOOK

For picking up dropped stitches (see page 28). Yes – even the most seasoned knitters still drop them.

6 TAPE MEASURE

For measuring your work. A small retractable tape measure is ideal and easy to stow in your project bag.

7 SCISSORS

For snipping yarn ends. Any will do – even kitchen scissors – but I use a small, sharp pair bought from my local haberdashery.

8 TAPESTRY NEEDLE

A blunt-ended needle with a large eye. It is used for sewing up knitted pieces and darning in loose yarn ends.

9 PINS

Any type of pin will do but large heads are helpful because they will not get lost in the knitted fabric.

10 STITCH HOLDER

These are like big safety pins and are used to store stitches securely when you are not using them. You could equally use a large safety pin if you don't have many stitches to keep safe.

11 PENCIL AND NOTEBOOK

If you don't have a row counter, a pencil and notebook are just as good for noting rows worked. They are also handy for noting any pattern changes and where you have got up to in the pattern.

12 STRAIGHT RULER

For accurately measuring your tension swatch on a flat surface.

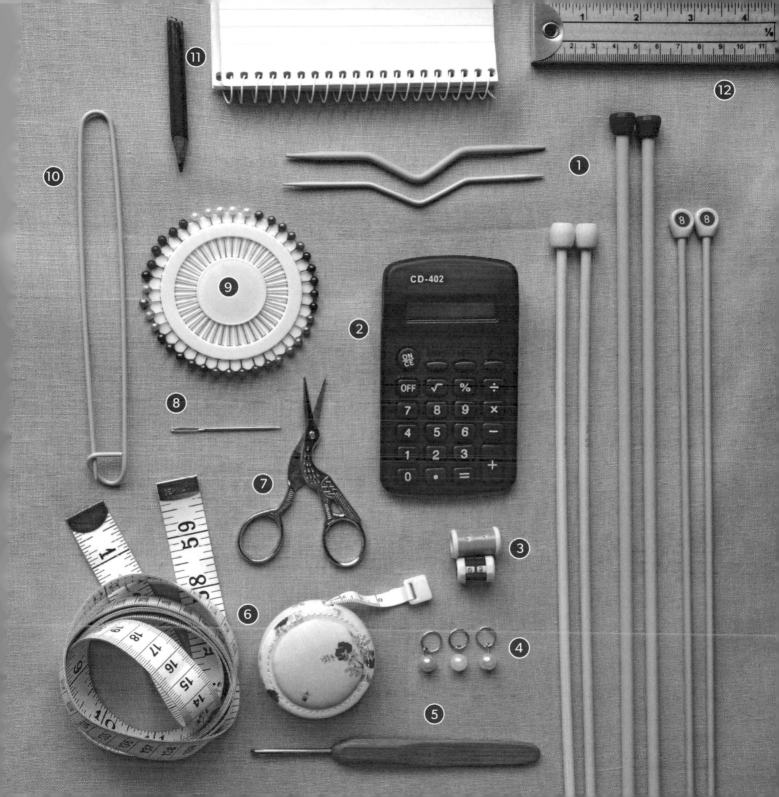

BASIC TECHNIQUES

HOLDING THE NEEDLES

Holding the needles (or live lobsters, because that is how they are likely to feel initially) is the first thing to practise. It may feel daunting to start with, but it will soon become more natural.

Just as there are two ways of knitting, the English method and the Continental method (see pages 36–9), there are two ways of holding the needles. Choose which method suits you best.

Tip If you are left-handed, I recommend you start by learning the Continental method because the main working needle and yarn are controlled with the left hand, which will be slightly easier for you.

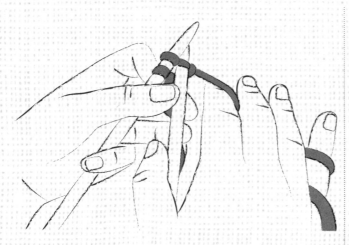

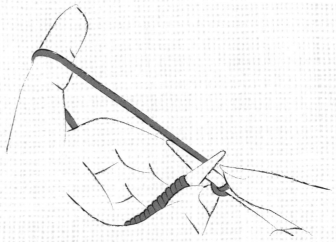

ENGLISH METHOD

Hold the needle with the stitches in your left hand. With the palm of your right hand facing you, wrap the yarn around your little finger, over the other fingers and then underneath your index finger. With the working needle in your right hand, control the tension of the yarn with your right index finger.

CONTINENTAL METHOD

Hold the needle with the stitches in your right hand. Wrap the yarn around your little finger and then around the index finger of your left hand. Move the needle holding the stitches into your left hand. With the working needle in your right hand, control the tension of the yarn with your left index finger.

MAKING A SLIP KNOT

Both methods of knitting will always begin with a slip knot.
From here you will begin to cast on the stitches that make the row.

1 Draw out about 4in (10cm) of yarn from the ball and cross over the strands to make a loop. Pull the strand attached to the ball through the loop to form a second loop. Place the new loop on the knitting needle.

2 Tighten the slip knot by pulling on both ends of the yarn.

Tip Initially, it may feel tricky to hold the needles and yarn exactly as the picture guides suggest. It is probably wise to try to follow the step-by-step guide from the get-go, but don't worry if you don't succeed; the most important part is getting to grips with the way the stitch is worked. After you become more fluent, you can fiddle about with hand and yarn position.

CASTING ON

There are two main methods for casting on. The knit-on method, also known as the cable cast-on, is the quickest and easiest to learn.

The thumb method (see facing page) is a little trickier but it gives a wonderfully elastic edge and looks especially neat and tidy.

THE KNIT-ON METHOD

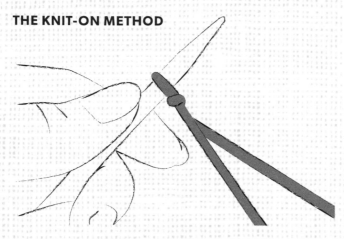

1 Make a slip knot (see page 19) a few inches (several cm) from the end of the yarn and place onto the needle. Pull the knot tight to make the first stitch.

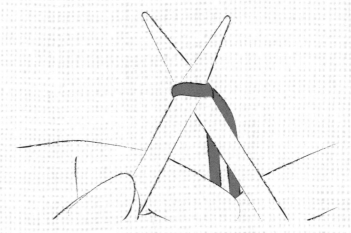

2 Hold the needle with the slip knot in your left hand. Push the point of the empty needle through the loop on the needle from front to back. Make sure the needles form a cross shape.

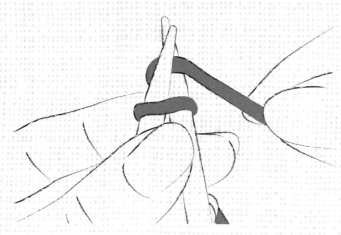

3 Wrap the yarn around the needle anti-clockwise and bring between the cross of the needles from front to back.

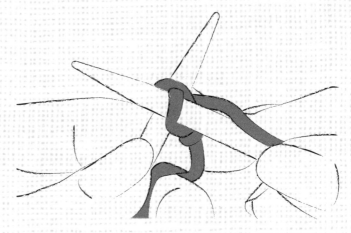

4 With the tip of the right-hand needle, pull the yarn back through the loop on the left-hand needle. Form a cross shape with the needles.

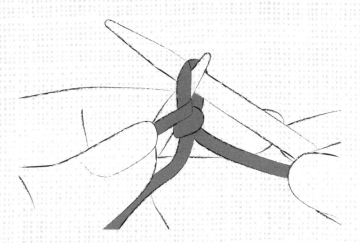

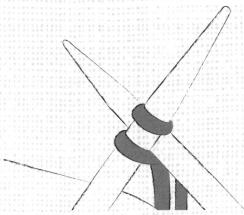

5 Place the new loop onto the tip of the left-hand needle and pull tight to make a stitch.

6 Insert your right-hand needle between the two stitches and repeat steps 3–5. Continue until you have the correct amount on your needles.

THUMB METHOD

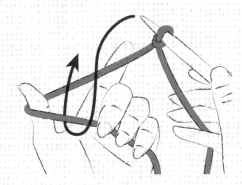

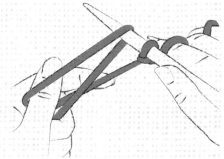

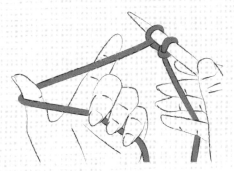

1 Make a slip knot (see page 19) approx 12in (30cm) from the end of the yarn. Hold the needle with the knot in your right hand. Wind the loose tail end of the yarn around the left thumb from front to back.

2 Insert the tip of the needle under the loop of yarn as shown. Using the ball end of the yarn wrapped over your right index finger, take this yarn over the tip of the needle.

3 Pull the loop made by the ball end of the yarn through the loop around the thumb, slipping the loop off the thumb and gently pulling the loose end to close the stitch.

CASTING OFF

There's just one method for casting off, which is quite straightforward.

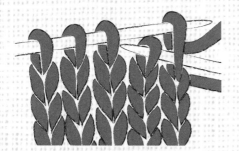

1 Knit the first two stitches. Push the point of the left needle through the first stitch on the right needle and lift it over the second stitch. One stitch remains on the right needle.

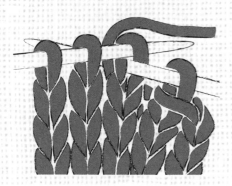

2 Knit another stitch from the left needle and repeat step 1. Repeat until you have one stitch left. Cut the yarn, leaving a long tail, thread it through the remaining stitch and pull tight.

TENSION

To knitters, tension refers to the number of stitches and rows to an inch or centimetre. At the start of each pattern there is always a section telling you exactly how many stitches and rows there should be over a set measurement, usually a 4in (10cm) square. Provided you use the yarn and needles stated, your tension will probably match this with only a slight variation, depending on whether you are a tight or loose knitter.

However, problems can arise if you substitute the stated yarn with another one. Even a yarn of a similar weight can vary in tension when knitted up. Therefore, you will need to check the stitch sizes match so the finished project will come out the correct size by making a tension swatch. This is especially important when knitting a garment, less so when knitting a project such as a cushion, where the finished size may be less crucial.

KNITTING A TENSION SWATCH

To knit a tension swatch, cast on 40 stitches using the recommended needle size. Work in pattern for at least 4in (10cm) before casting off loosely. Lay the swatch out on a flat surface and place a flat ruler vertically on top. Count the number of rows over 4in (10cm). Then do the same horizontally but this time count the number of stitches over 4in (10cm).

If you have more stitches and rows than stated on the pattern, knit the tension swatch again using larger needles.

If you have fewer stitches and rows, repeat with smaller needles. Try working with different needles until your tension matches that of the pattern.

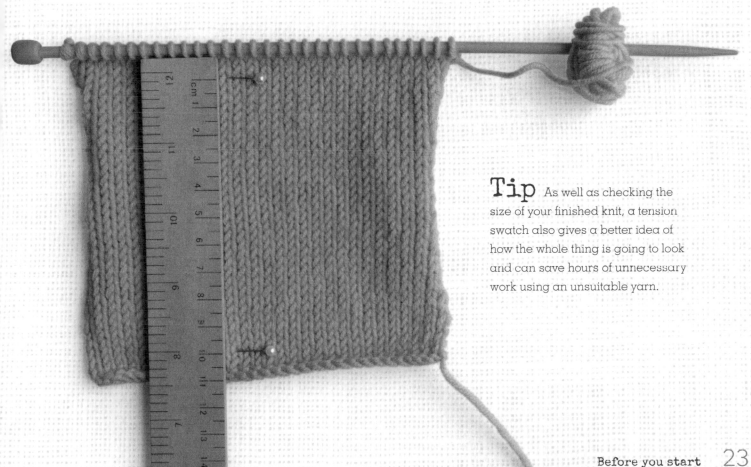

Tip As well as checking the size of your finished knit, a tension swatch also gives a better idea of how the whole thing is going to look and can save hours of unnecessary work using an unsuitable yarn.

HOW TO FOLLOW A
KNITTING PATTERN

Before you begin knitting, always read
the pattern through from beginning to
end. Figures for larger sizes are given
in round brackets and where only one
figure appears, this applies to all sizes.
For example, if you are knitting a sweater
that offers a choice of sizes, you may read
the instruction: 'Using 3.25mm needles,
cast on 97[103:109:115:119] sts.' Choose
the size you want to knit and mark it
throughout the pattern with a highlighter
or pencil. This will make it easier to follow
the instructions for the correct size.

Next, check that you understand
all of the abbreviations; the ones used
in this book are listed on page 33.

It is useful to know that all patterns
follow a conventional format. There
may be slight variations in style but
the same information will always be
given, including the materials used, sizes,
tension, pattern instructions and
finishing instructions.

SCHEMATICS

Patterns may also include a schematic,
which is a flat map of the project with
key measurements marked on it. This
can be a handy visual reference for
you. If you want to alter any elements
of the pattern, such as the sleeve
length, you can see where these
changes should be made.

DARNING IN LOOSE ENDS

Attached to every piece of finished knitting are long yarn tails hanging along the side edges. If you are knitting in stripes, you may find there are even more tails than usual. To tidy them up, you should darn them into the fabric.

Thread the yarn end through the tapestry needle. Working on the wrong side of the fabric, bring the yarn in and out of the bumps made by the stitches along the neighbouring rows about four or five times. Snip the yarn close to the end.

Tip Don't worry if your work looks lumpy and untidy after darning in the yarn ends. Simply block and press the piece according to the instructions on page 26. It will transform the knitting and, like magic, the lumps and bumps will smooth out and the stitches will even up and become neat and tidy.

JOINING PIECES TOGETHER

BLOCKING AND PRESSING

Once you have knitted all the pieces of your project, you need to put them together. After you have darned in all the loose yarn tails (see page 25), you will need to block (stretch) and press your pieces into shape. This will help the stitches to lie beautifully, unroll the edges (if you have been working in stocking stitch), stretch out lace stitches and help the task of sewing up run more smoothly.

Firstly, check your ball band. Each yarn will carry instructions on whether it is suitable to be pressed with an iron and at what temperature.

PRESSING

If your yarn is suitable for pressing with an iron, use a damp tea towel or cloth between the iron and the knitted fabric. Never apply direct heat to your knitting.

PINNING AND BLOCKING

If your yarn is not suitable for pressing, or you have knitted a piece of lace (see information in box on right), you will need to pin and block the piece into shape. Wet your piece in lukewarm water. Do not agitate it; you need to make it damp but you're not washing it. Gently squeeze out the excess water and lay it on a flat surface on a towel to absorb the moisture. Now carefully stretch the piece into shape and secure it in place on the towel with pins. Leave to dry or use steam from an iron to gently finish the drying process.

WHY BLOCK LACE KNITTING?

After finishing any lace knitting project, you will find that your work looks nothing like the photograph in the pattern. You may have anticipated a beautiful, complex, cobweb-like garment; however, you will inevitably end up with a thin, rolled-up tube of netting.

The magic happens only after you have blocked your knitting. Follow the instructions on this page, making sure you stretch the piece to the measurements given on the pattern and you will transform your work into everything you hoped it would be.

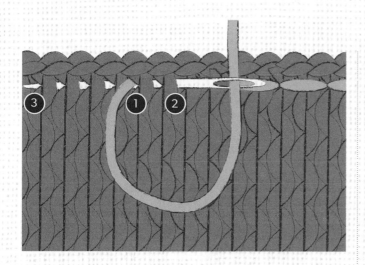

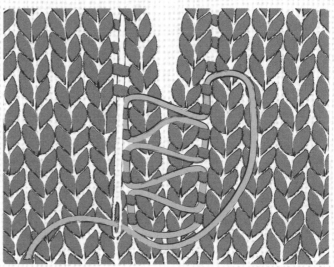

SEAMING WITH BACK STITCH

One of the simplest ways to join two pieces of knitted fabric is by using back stitch.

Work from right to left. Bring the needle up to the right side of work at point 1, down at point 2 and back up at 3. Try to keep the distance between stitches even. Begin next stitch at point 1. Repeat until the seam is complete. To finish off, make a few small invisible stitches in the fabric. Cut yarn.

SEAMING WITH MATTRESS STITCH

When you need a flat, invisible seam, mattress stitch is the best. The technique may feel slightly trickier at first than back stitch but once you get used to it, it is really very straightforward. For invisible seams, always sew pieces together using matching yarn.

Place pieces to be joined side by side on a flat surface with the right side facing towards you. Take a threaded needle and secure it to the fabric by weaving down the side edge of one of the pieces. Bring the needle out between the first and second stitches. Working vertically, insert the needle at the back of the opposite piece, bring out at the front and insert into the first row again from front to back, bringing it up below the horizontal strand. Go back to the first piece and keep stitching in the same way. You will see your stitches form a ladder along the seam. Pull the yarn tight every few stitches to close the fabric neatly.

Tip Blocking your knitted pieces is going to make seaming so much easier. The edges will behave and lay nice and flat so you can see exactly what you are doing and where to put your needle.

TROUBLESHOOTING

Inevitably, there will come a time when a stitch will be dropped off the needle. We have all done it and still do. Do not hurl everything across the room in terror as I used to do. Stay calm, even if the stitch is unravelling down the rows and leaving a big ladder. Reach for a crochet hook and follow the guidance provided below.

PICKING UP A DROPPED STITCH

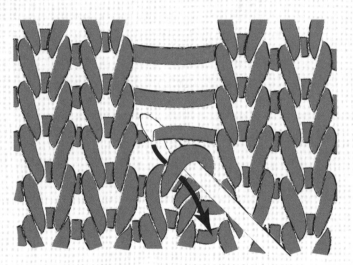 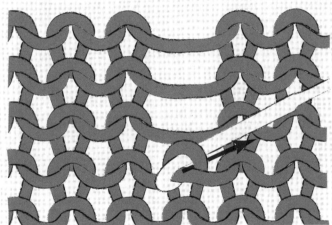

ON A KNIT ROW

Knit along the row until you reach the dropped stitch. Make sure the dropped stitch is sitting at the front of the work and in front of the horizontal ladders. Put the tip of the crochet hook into the loop of the dropped stitch from front to back and then, using the hook, catch the horizontal strand and pull it through the stitch. The strand has now become a stitch. Repeat as many times as necessary until the dropped stitch has been picked up through all the rungs of the ladder to the top. Place back on left-hand needle.

ON A PURL ROW

Purl along the row to the dropped stitch. Make sure the dropped stitch is sitting at the back of the work behind the horizontal ladders. Put the tip of the crochet hook into the loop of the dropped stitch from back to front and then, using the hook, catch the horizontal strand and pull it through the stitch. The strand has now become a stitch. Repeat as many times as necessary until the dropped stitch has been picked up through all the rungs of the ladder to the top. Place back on left-hand needle.

UNDOING ONE ROW

If you spot a mistake only a few stitches along the row you are currently working on, you can carefully pick your way back along the stitches to correct it.

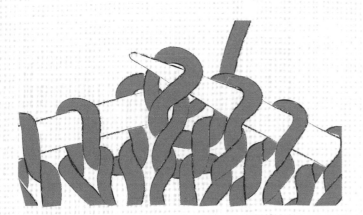

ON A KNIT ROW

With the yarn at the back, pick up the stitch by inserting the left-hand needle from front to back into the stitch below the free loop. Drop the stitch above off the needle and pull the working yarn, withdrawing the stitch loop.

ON A PURL ROW

With the yarn in front, pick up the stitch by inserting the left-hand needle from front to back into the stitch below the free loop. Drop the stitch above off the needle and pull the working yarn, withdrawing the stitch loop.

UNRAVELLING YOUR WORK

Sometimes the unthinkable happens and you are several rows on before you notice a mistake in the pattern. You'll need to unravel your work until you reach the mistake so you can correct it. This may seem terrifying, but you can manage it with care. Slide the stitches off your needle and gently pull the yarn so the stitches unravel row by row. Do this slowly and carefully until you are a few rows below your mistake. Put the stitches back onto your needle, beginning with those furthest away from the working yarn. Once you have picked up all the stitches, continue knitting the pattern as before.

ADVICE FOR LEFT-HANDED KNITTERS

All knitting patterns are written for right-handers but do not be put off by this. There are two options you might consider.

Do you definitely want to knit left-handed? If the answer is yes, then try the Continental method of knitting (see page 38), which you may find easier to master. The English method primarily uses the right hand and the right-hand needle to make the stitches whereas the left-hand needle and left hand dominate when using the Continental method. I know left-handed people who find this technique far easier and quicker.

If, however, you are set on mastering the English method of knitting, you will need to work all the steps in the Knit Stitch and the Purl Stitch sections (pages 36–7 and 42–3) in reverse, holding your working needle in your left hand instead of your right. This is a little complicated but not impossible to do. You might find it helpful to use a mirror to reverse your hands and make things easier.

One left-handed lady I knew assured me that she would learn to knit right handed and if she did this from the get-go, she would not find it clumsy. True to her word, she did master things this way. Rest assured that everyone – both right- and left-handers   feel clumsy and awkward as they begin knitting, so perseverance and practice is the key in all cases.

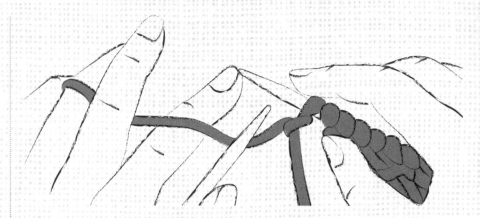

When working the knit stitch, hold the needle with the live stitches in your right hand and the empty needle (the working needle) in your left hand. Insert the working needle into the first stitch on the right-hand needle from front to back.

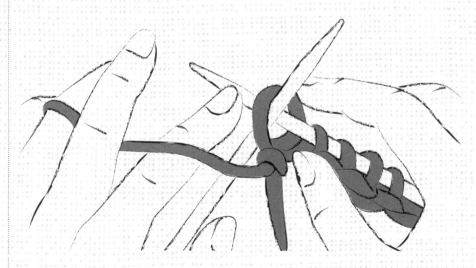

When working the purl stitch, hold the needle with the live stitches in your right hand and the empty needle (the working needle) in your left hand. Insert the working needle into the first stitch on the right-hand needle from back to front.

CARING FOR YOUR KNITS

After having taken such love and care knitting your project, you will want to take the same care when washing it. Always check the ball band of the yarn to see which washing method is recommended. For instance, a garment made in 100% pure wool might felt and shrink if washed in the machine at high temperature. In this instance, gentle hand washing in warm or cool water would be suitable.

These days, there are more and more yarns on the market (mostly a mix of wool and man-made fibres) that can be machine washed, especially those designed for children's knits. These could be the perfect choice if you don't have free time to spend at the sink hand washing.

However you wash your garment, take care to dry it flat on an absorbent surface such as a towel to soak up excess moisture. Don't be tempted to chuck it in a tumble dryer or hang it over a radiator. Dry it flat and ease it into shape.

When the garment is dry, it should look fine. If you feel it needs further pressing, check the ball band before applying any direct heat. Usually, most fibres require a little gentle steam or very gentle pressing.

Tip When pressing your knits use a damp cloth between the knitted fabric and the iron.

KNITTING NEEDLE CONVERSION CHART

UK	Metric	US	UK	Metric	US
14	2mm	0	6	5mm	8
13	2.25mm	1	5	5.5mm	9
12	2.75mm	2	4	6mm	10
11	3mm	–	3	6.5mm	10.5
10	3.25mm	3	2	7mm	10.5
–	3.5mm	4	1	7.5mm	11
9	3.75mm	5	0	8mm	11
8	4mm	6	00	9mm	13
7	4.5mm	7	000	10mm	15

UK/US YARN WEIGHT CONVERSION CHART

UK	US
4-ply	sport
double knitting	light worsted
Aran	fisherman/worsted
chunky	bulky
super chunky	extra bulky

ABBREVIATIONS

Here are the abbreviations used in this book, plus some others that are commonly used.

( )	work instructions within brackets as many times as directed
alt	alternate
approx	approximately
beg	beginning
C4b	cable 4 back: slip next 2 stitches onto cable needle and hold at back of work, knit 2 stitches, then knit 2 stitches from cable needle
C4f	cable 4 front: slip next 2 stitches onto cable needle and hold at back of work, knit 2 stitches, then knit 2 stitches from cable needle
CC	contrast colour
cm	centimetre
Cn	cable needle
CO	cast on
cont	continue
dec	decrease
DK	double-knitting weight yarn
foll	following
g	grams
g st	garter stitch

inc	increase
ins	inches
k	knit
k2tog	decrease by knitting 2 sts together
kfb	increase by knitting into front and back of next st
LH	left hand
MC	main colour
meas	measures
P	purl
P2tog	decrease by purling 2 sts together
patt	pattern
rem	remaining
rep	repeat
RH	right hand
RS	right side
st(s)	stitch(es)
st st	stocking stitch
tog	together
WS	wrong side
yo	yarn over

TECHNIQUES
& PROJECTS

THE KNIT STITCH

WE COVERED CASTING-ON STITCHES ON PAGE 20, SO YOU HAVE ALREADY CREATED LIVE STITCHES ON YOUR NEEDLES. NOW COMES THE EXCITING BIT: KNITTING YOUR FIRST ROW. I AM BEGINNING WITH THE KNIT STITCH, WHICH HAS ALWAYS BEEN THE FIRST STITCH LEARNT BY NOVICE KNITTERS.

The beauty of knitting is that every single stitch variation is only ever a combination of just two stitches: knit or purl. We will go on to learn about the purl stitch later but for now we will concentrate on the beautiful knit stitch.

Note that the knit stitch can also be called by several different names; for instance, you may have heard it referred to as a 'plain' stitch or 'garter' stitch. Please don't be concerned by this at all;

it is just a slight difference in terminology. I will refer to it as the 'knit' stitch to keep things simple.

There are two basic ways to create the knit stitch: English or Continental style. I have always used the English method, simply because this is the way I was taught by my gran, but I have lots of friends who knit using the Continental method. Both methods are equally as efficient and simple; they vary only in whether you

hold the end of the yarn in your left hand or right hand. You may like to experiment with both methods to see which feels more comfortable, or you may choose one style and stick with that. If you are left handed, however, I suggest you start with the Continental method (see page 38) since you hold the yarn in the left hand and knit with the right, which you may find easier than trying to use the English method and reversing the hands.

Tip There are four basic steps to working the knit stitch using the English method: in, over, under and off – or as one of my students used to say: stab it, wrap it, go under and yank it off!

ENGLISH METHOD

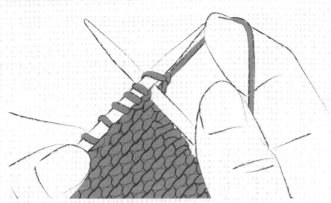

1 Hold the needle with the stitches in your left hand. Place your hand on top firmly but not too tightly. With your right hand, hold the yarn behind the work. Insert the point of the empty needle into the front of the first stitch as shown.

2 Wrap the yarn anti-clockwise around the point of the right hand needle using your index finger. Try to keep the yarn taut but not too tight so that your tension will be nice and even as you go along.

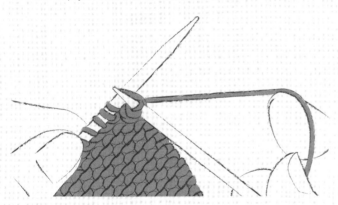

3 Bring the right-hand needle back through the loop towards you, moving under the left-hand needle and making sure to catch the yarn you already wound, bringing it with you to the front of the work.

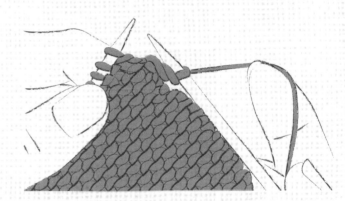

4 Now pull the original stitch off the tip of the left-hand needle and onto the right-hand needle. You have created your first knit stitch. Now work steps 1–4 across the row on every stitch until all the new stitches have been transferred from the left needle to the right needle. For the next row, swap the needles around so that your finished row is in your left hand and your empty needle is in your right. Work each step again as you did before.

CONTINENTAL METHOD

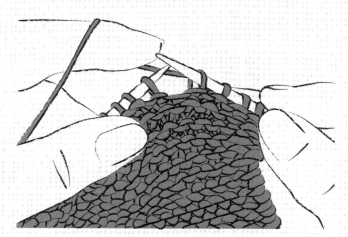

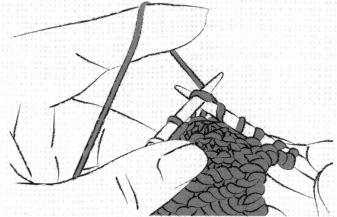

1 Wind the yarn around your left little finger and over your left index finger. Pick up the needle with the stitches on and hold it in your left hand. Keep your index finger (with the yarn wrapped around it) pointing in the air so the yarn is kept taut and even.

2 Slide the point of the right-hand needle through the front of the first loop on the left-hand needle from front to back. Your needles will make an 'x' shape.

3 Hook the tip of the right-hand needle under the strand of yarn wrapped around your index finger, scooping it up in readiness for step 4.

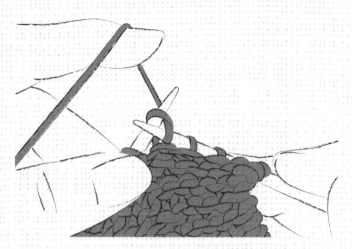

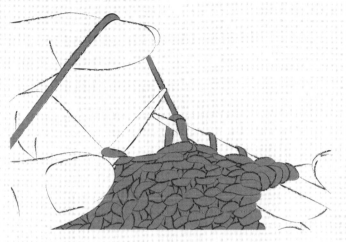

4 Pull this new loop back out of the loop you came in from and under the right-hand needle. You will be doing all the work with the right-hand needle, almost picking the stitches from the strand around your index finger and pulling the new loops back under to the front of your work. Once the loop is at the front of the work, slide the right-hand needle upwards so the needles make an 'x' shape again.

5 Pull the old loop off the needle. Carefully work steps 1–5 across the row on every stitch until all the new stitches have been transferred from the left-hand needle to the right-hand needle. For the next row, swap the needles around so that your finished row is in your left hand and your empty needle is in your right. Work each step again as you did before.

Tip Here are a couple of rhymes to help you remember how to work this stitch:

For English Method:
In through the front door,
Once around the back,
Peek through the window,
And off jumps Jack.

For Continental Method:
In through the front door,
Up over the back,
Peek through the window,
And off jumps Jack.

TABLET COVER

IT IS EASY TO CREATE THIS STYLISH TABLET COVER USING JUST THE KNIT STITCH. GET TO GRIPS WITH THE STITCH ITSELF USING THE STEP-BY-STEP GUIDE ON PAGES 36–9 BEFORE MOVING ON TO KNIT TWO SIMPLE SQUARES, WHICH ARE JOINED TO MAKE AN ATTRACTIVE POCKET.

YOU WILL NEED

Blacker Yarns Swan DK 100% Falkland Islands merino (119yd/110m per 50g ball):
2 balls Pale Fawn Sand
1 pair 4mm (US6:UK8) needles
Scissors
Tapestry needle
20in (50cm) leather thong or ribbon
Sewing needle and thread to match yarn
Large decorative button
Beads to decorate ends (optional)

TENSION

20 sts and 38 rows to 4in (10cm) over g st using 4mm needles.
Use larger or smaller needles if necessary to obtain correct tension.

FINISHED SIZE

7⅓in x 9½in (19cm x 24cm)

TECHNIQUES USED

Knit stitch (see page 36)
Darning in loose ends (see page 25)
Joining seams (see page 27)

INSTRUCTIONS

FRONT AND BACK (BOTH ALIKE)

Using 4mm needles and either the knit-on or thumb method, cast on 45 sts.
Row 1 (RS): Knit.
This row forms the garter st pattern.
Rep this row until work meas 19in (24cm).
Cast off.
Work another piece exactly the same as the first.

Tip When a pattern tells you to knit every row, this may also be referred to as garter stitch (g st). It simply means 'knit every row'.

FINISHING

1 Darn in loose yarn ends.
2 Place one square on top of the other. Using a tapestry needle and a length of fawn yarn, join the two longer side seams and the bottom short seam.
3 Using a sewing needle and thread, sew the button onto the centre of the front of the cover approx 1in (2.5cm) down from the open edge.
4 Cut 2 lengths of leather thong or ribbon approx 4in (10cm) long and attach beads to one end of each piece.
5 Using a sewing needle and thread, sew both pieces to the centre back opening of the cover. Flip the thongs to the front and knot together to fit over the button.

THE PURL STITCH

THERE ARE ONLY TWO STITCHES TO LEARN IN KNITTING, AND ONCE YOU HAVE LEARNT THEM BOTH, YOU ARE EQUIPPED TO WORK ANY OF THE DIFFERENT STITCH PATTERNS THAT EXIST. YOU HAVE ALREADY CONQUERED THE KNIT STITCH AND NOW IT IS TIME TO LEARN THE PURL STITCH.

The purl stitch is much maligned; seemingly always destined to feature on the back of your work and never on the front, where the real show is going on. And initially it will seem a little harder to master than the knit stitch. However, if you keep in mind that the humble purl stitch is merely a knit stitch worked in reverse, this may help you as you master the second and last stitch in your repertoire.

Firstly, let me explain what the purl stitch looks like and how it affects the finished look of its partner, the knit stitch. The knit stitch, when repeated row after row, produces a bumpy, ridge fabric – garter stitch. If you worked the purl stitch row after row, this too would produce a similar ridged fabric that would look very much like the garter-stitch version.

The magic really happens when you combine the two stitches. If you work one row in knit stitch and then one row in purl stitch, the front of the work (the knit side) will form a smooth, draped fabric with a series of 'v' shapes all across it. The reverse side (the purl side) will be bumpy just like garter stitch. We call this pattern stocking stitch and it is arguably one of the most universally used stitches across the craft of knitting.

There is another element to the combination of knit and purl stitches. If you use a purl stitch on the right side (the knit side) of your stocking-stitch pattern, it will leave a bump. Designers like to call this bump effect 'texture'. So if you make a few bumps in strategic places along the right side of stocking stitch, you can make an attractive and textured piece of knitted fabric.

So, instead of thinking of the purl stitch as the annoying tricky stitch you have to get around to learning, focus on it more like a gateway into endless creative knitting opportunities.

Take your time and work through the instructions for purl. As for the knit stitch, I have included both the English and Continental methods of working this stitch. Again, if you are left-handed, it may be easier to try to learn the Continental method first (see page 44).

ENGLISH METHOD

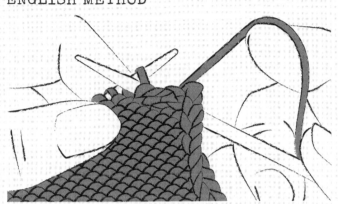

1 Hold your yarn and needles in exactly the same way as you would for the knit stitch, with the yarn in the right hand. However, instead of holding the yarn at the back of the work as you did with the knit stitch, the yarn stays at the front while working the purl stitch. Insert the right-hand needle into the front of the stitch from right to left.

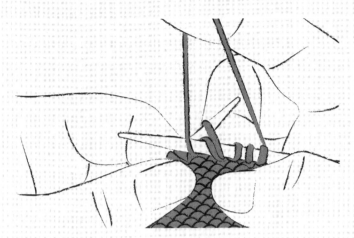

2 Pass the yarn over and around the right-hand needle from back to front.

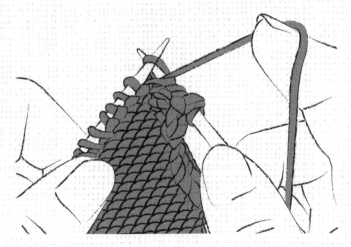

3 Holding the yarn down between the two needles, slide the right-hand needle down the base of the left-hand needle, pushing the point of the right needle, with its new loop, out through the back of the stitch you came in at.

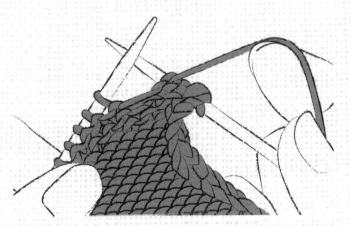

4 Slip the stitch off the tip of the left needle. That is one stitch completed. Now complete steps 1–4 again to complete your first purl row.

CONTINENTAL METHOD

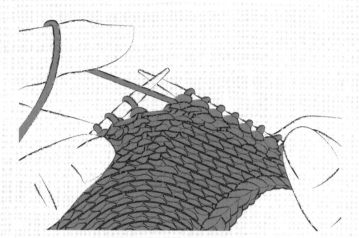

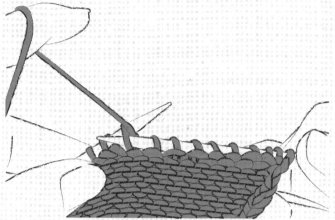

1 Hold your yarn and needles in the same way you would to make the knit stitch, holding the yarn in your left hand. But as for the English method of making a purl stitch, the yarn will stay at the front of the work all along the row.

2 Insert the right-hand needle into the front of the stitch from right to left, keeping the yarn at the front of the work.

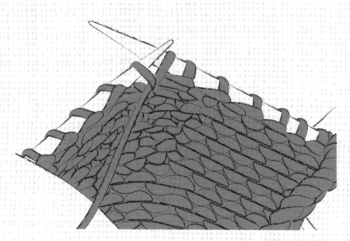

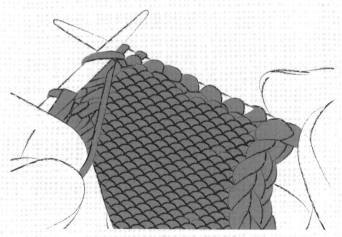

3 Bring the yarn in your left hand around the tip of the right needle in an anti-clockwise motion. Then bring your left index finger, with the yarn around it, down between the two needles.

4 Keeping the yarn in this position, carefully slide the right needle down the base of the left needle. Push the tip of the needle out through the back of the stitch you came in through.

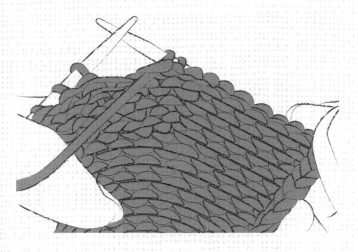

5 Slip the stitch off the tip of the left needle and return your index finger back to its original position above the needle. Repeat steps 1–5 all along the row.

Tip If you put your knitting down and forget which row comes next, pick it up as if you are ready to begin again. Look at the side facing you. If it is smooth with little 'v' shapes all over it, your next row is a knit one. If it is bumpy, you will know it is a purl row next.

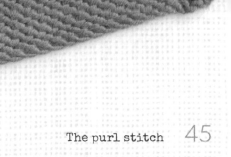

HOT-WATER BOTTLE COVER

THIS LUXURY HOT-WATER BOTTLE COVER HAS NO TRICKY SHAPING TO WORRY ABOUT SO YOU
CAN SIMPLY PRACTISE YOUR KNIT AND PURL ROWS TO CREATE A STOCKING-STITCH PATTERN.
EMBELLISH THE COVER WITH BUTTONS AND RIBBON TO MAKE IT REALLY SPECIAL.

YOU WILL NEED

Blacker Yarns Pure Blue-faced Leicester
DK (119yd/110m per 50g ball)
2 balls
1 pair 4mm (US6:UK8) needles
Scissors
20in (50cm) cream satin ribbon
10 large and 10 small mother-of-pearl
buttons
Sewing needle and cream thread

TENSION

20 sts and 28 rows to 4in (10cm) over st st
using 4mm needles.
Use larger or smaller needles if necessary
to obtain correct tension.

FINISHED SIZE

14in x 8in (36cm x 20cm)

TECHNIQUES USED

Knit stitch (see page 36)
Purl stitch (see page 42)
Darning in loose ends (see page 25)
Joining seams (see page 27)

INSTRUCTIONS

COVER

Using 4mm needles, cast on 85 sts.
Row 1 (RS): Knit.
Row 2 (WS): Purl.
These 2 rows form the stocking
stitch pattern.
Rep these 2 rows until work meas
11in (28cm) ending on a Row 2.
Knit every row (garter st) for a further
3in (8cm).

FINISHING

1 Darn in loose yarn ends.
2 Fold cover in half lengthwise with
   RS facing.
3 Join the long side seam using
   mattress stitch.
4 Place the cover on a hard surface and
   flatten it, making sure the seam lies to
   one side. Sew the bottom, cast-on edge
   seam so you have a rectangular pocket.
5 Turn RS out and pop your hot-water
   bottle inside. Tie the ribbon around the
   neck of the bottle.
6 Position the buttons randomly around
   the front of your bottle. When you are
   happy with their position, sew on firmly
   with the sewing needle and cotton.

Tips
You could also work this cover using the knit stitch only.
Knit every row to make garter stitch. For a different look, make a plaited
or twisted cord instead of using ribbon and add pompoms to each end.

CHANGING COLOURS

ONE OF THE SIMPLEST AND EASIEST WAYS TO ADD COLOUR TO YOUR KNITTING IS BY ALTERNATING YOUR PALETTE USING STRIPES. HERE YOU WILL FIND OUT HOW TO JOIN A NEW COLOUR AND HOW TO CARRY THE COLOUR YOU ARE NOT USING ALONGSIDE YOUR WORK.

The straightforward horizontal stripe is so versatile and can be a great creative tool for your knitting projects. It can be cool and chic, as in the classic Breton sweater; fun, bright and playful (see Kenzo or Sonia Rykiel for inspiration); or, like the Hobo Bag I have designed to accompany this section, subtle with toning shades of the same colour.

Stripes can be wide or narrow, have regular combinations of colour repeats or more eclectic, mixed-up repeats. You can work them however you like. It's a great way to develop your artistic side and get to know how colours can work together as a team.

So, what do you need to know before you start? Firstly, whenever you are working in stocking stitch and you need to join a new colour, you must plan so you are at the beginning of a knit row, i.e. the right side of your work, before you start. If you join the new colour when beginning the purl row, the join will show on the front of the work and look untidy. Therefore, it is best

to make sure you have an even number of rows in between each stripe so you will be at the correct side of the work when you next need to change colour.

Secondly, you need to decide what to do with the old yarn colour. You can cut the unused yarn from the project whenever you change to a new colour. This method is simple but leaves a yarn tail that you will need to sew in neatly when finishing your piece. And when you come to finishing your work, you may well end up with lots of yarn ends to sew in to the edges. I call this the cut and tie method. If you find finishing off a bit of a chore, try the weaving-in method, which involves weaving the new tail end into your knitting as you work the first few stitches. Then you either snip the excess yarn or carry the unused colours up the side of your work as you go – without snipping. This technique is a little trickier but will reduce the amount of sewing at the end.

Tip If you decide to change colour while working rib, always knit the first row in the new colour and then return to the rib pattern for the second row. This will give a much neater effect and a sharper appearance to your stripes on the right side of your work.

THE CUT AND TIE METHOD

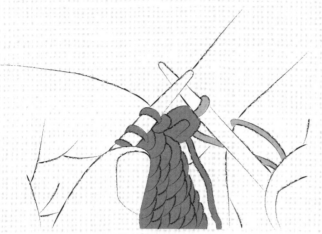

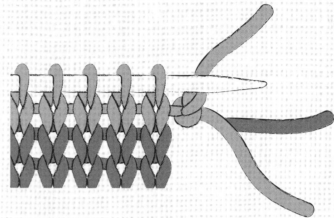

1 With the RS facing you and the next row being a knit one, take your new colour and knit the first few stitches with it.

2 *Optional:* Snip the old colour you are no longer using (or leave it and carry it up the edge of the work as detailed right). Tie both tail ends together and continue to knit the end of the row. (Note the tail ends at the beginning of the row.)

Experiment with colour combinations using this simple method.

Tip If you are planning your own combination of stripes and are not sure if the colours will work together, take a ruler and wrap it with the colours you would like to use. Wrap thick and thin sections to work out how wide to make your stripes. Wrap different colour combinations beside each other to see how they dominate or harmonize. It eliminates some of the risk before you begin your project and can save you the agony of unravelling a combination you suddenly find you dislike.

THE WEAVING-IN METHOD

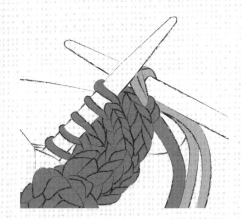 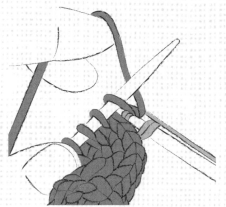 

1 With the RS facing you and the next row being a knit one, take your new colour and knit the first stitch with it, making sure you leave a tail end of about 2in (2.5cm).

2 Knit the second stitch but twist the yarn around the tail end as you go. Repeat for at least five stitches.

3 With the WS facing you, snip the excess yarn and continue knitting across the row. Optional: either snip the old colour away or carry it up with you as detailed below.

CARRYING THE COLOURS ALONGSIDE YOUR WORK

When you return to the beginning of the knit row after working a row of purl, pass the working yarn under the yarns not being used at the side edge of the work. Knit the next row. Repeat these two rows. All the unused colours will sit in a nice twist at the side edge of your work. At the moment they are needed, they will be sitting right at the beginning of the next knit row.

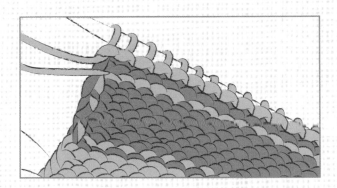

STRIPED HOBO BAG

CREATING THIS FUNKY BAG IS REALLY STRAIGHTFORWARD. I'VE CHOSEN TO USE AN ARAN WEIGHT YARN SO THE PROJECT WILL GROW QUICKLY. IT WILL LOOK IMPRESSIVE ALTHOUGH THE CONSTRUCTION IS SIMPLE – ALL YOU DO IS KNIT TWO STRIPED SQUARES AND A LONG STRIP.

YOU WILL NEED

Artesano Aran 50% alpaca, 50% wool
(144yd/132m per 100g hank)
2 hanks in Mahogany (A)
1 hank in Walnut (B)
1 hank in Birch (C)
1 pair 5mm (US8:UK6) needles
Scissors
Pins
Tapestry needle
Snap fastener
Sewing needle and matching
sewing thread

TENSION

17 sts and 21 rows to 4in (10cm) over st st
using 5mm needles.
Use larger or smaller needles if necessary
to obtain correct tension.

FINISHED SIZE

14in x 13in (36cm x 33cm)

TECHNIQUES USED

Knit stitch (see page 36)
Purl stitch (see page 42)
Joining colours to make stripes
(see page 48)
Darning in loose yarn ends (see page 25)
Joining seams (see page 27)

INSTRUCTIONS

FRONT AND BACK (BOTH ALIKE)

Using 5mm needles and A, cast on 58 sts.
Row 1 (RS): Knit.
Row 2 (WS): Purl.
These 2 rows form stocking stitch.
Cont in st st and at same time work the
stripe patt as folls:
Work 4 rows A.
Work 4 rows B.
Work 4 rows C.
Rep the 12 rows of the stripe patt 5 times
(60 rows total).
Change to A.
Knit 4 rows in garter st.
Cast off.

FINISHING

1 Darn in loose yarn ends.
2 Join the short ends of the strap to make one loop.
3 Place first striped piece on a flat surface, RS facing downwards and with the cast-on edge nearest to you. Take the strap and find the seam. Position the seam at the centre of the cast-on edge of the striped piece and pin.
4 Lay the strap out evenly around the remaining lower and two side edges. Pin in place.
5 Sew the strap to the three edges of the striped rectangle with neat back stitches.
6 Turn the bag over and pin the second rectangle in place around the opposite edge of the strap, mirroring the first piece. Sew the strap to the three edges of this piece.
7 Sew a snap fastener to the inside of the garter-stitch edge at the top of the bag in the centre.

THE RIB STITCH

YOU HAVE TACKLED THE STOCKING STITCH AND ARE MAKING BRILLIANT PROGRESS, BUT YOU MAY
HAVE NOTICED THAT WHILE THE STOCKING STITCH IS SMOOTH AND HAS A WONDERFUL DRAPE,
IT DOES TEND TO CURL UP AT THE EDGES. THIS IS WHERE THE RIB STITCH COMES IN.

Like stocking stitch, the rib stitch is a combination of knit and purl stitches. This time, we are going to alternate the knit and purl stitches along every row to form ribbing, which looks like columns of smooth and bumpy stitches. The knit columns will stand out nice and smoothly at the front while the purl columns will sink into the back of the fabric, pulling the knit columns together so you hardly see the purl ones at all.

In this way, the fabric becomes very stretchy and can be used where you want the knitting to hug your body, as in cuffs, waists, sock tops and polo necks. In addition, ribbing does not curl at the edges. It stays flat, so it is also useful for scarves or blankets where you'd prefer not to have a rolled edge.

Knitting the rib stitch will also increase your aerobic capacity because it entails more arm action than the stocking stitch.

Remember how the yarn stayed at the back of the work during the knit stitch and then at the front of the work for the purl stitch? Well, if you are working both stitches along one row, you will have to keep bringing the yarn back and forth numerous times to accommodate the combination of the two.

To add to the challenge, there are many different types of rib stitch patterns. All are a combination of knit and purl and all are stretchy, but the variable factor is the number of stitches you are knitting and purling. You will still end up with columns of stitches but they may be narrower or wider depending on the combination.

I will explain the commonest forms of the rib stitch: single rib and double rib. Both are used in the following project.

Other variations of rib stitch can include stitch combinations such as k3, p1 (top), k2, p2 (bottom left) and k1, p1 (bottom right), all of which give a slightly different appearance.

SINGLE RIB STITCH

In a knitting pattern, single rib stitch will be written as '(k1, p1) rep to end of row'. To practise this, start by casting on 28 stitches and follow steps 1–3 below.

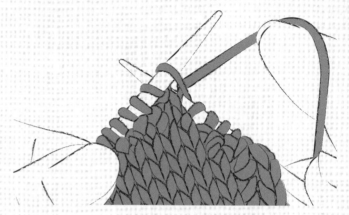

1   With the yarn at the back of your work, knit the first stitch as normal (see page 36).

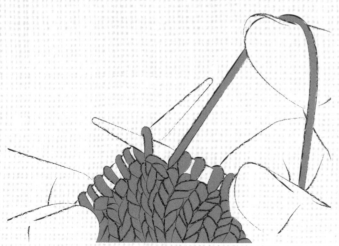

2   Bring the yarn to the front of the work between the tips of the two needles. Purl the next stitch.

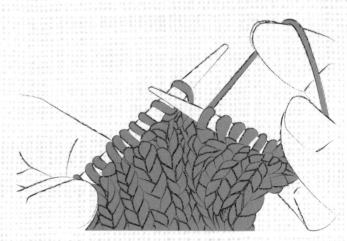

3   Take the yarn to the back of the work again and knit the next stitch. Repeat step 2 and then step 1 again to the end of the row. Repeat the row to make a single-rib stitch pattern.

DOUBLE RIB STITCH

The double rib stitch is worked in the same way as the single rib but you will work 2 knit stitches, bring the yarn to the front of the work to purl 2 stitches and then bring the yarn to the back of the work ready for another 2 knit stitches.

To practise double rib stitch, cast on 28 stitches and follow steps 1–3 for single rib stitch, but knit and then purl two stitches each time instead of one.

Tip

The action of moving the yarn back and forth between the needles can loosen the tension of the knitting somewhat. To compensate for this, ribbed knitting is often worked on needles that are two sizes smaller than for the stocking stitch in the pattern. This also ensures a firm but stretchy finish.

FINGERLESS GAUNTLETS

WOULD YOU BELIEVE THESE STYLISH FINGERLESS GAUNTLETS ARE MERE RECTANGLES OF RIBBED FABRIC? THAT IS THE BEAUTY OF THE RIB STITCH; ITS ELASTICITY MEANS IT HUGS WHERE IT TOUCHES, REMOVING THE NEED FOR COMPLICATED SHAPING. YOU CAN DECORATE THE GAUNTLETS WITH BUTTONS FOR EXTRA DETAIL.

YOU WILL NEED

2 x 50g balls or 1 x 100g ball of any DK weight yarn
1 pair 4mm (US6:UK8) needles
Tapestry needle
Scissors
Decorative buttons (optional)
Sewing needle and matching thread if sewing on buttons

TENSION

22 sts and 30 rows to 4in (10cm) over st st using 4mm needles.
Use larger or smaller needles if necessary to obtain correct tension.

FINISHED SIZE

To fit an average-sized woman's hands: length 13in (33cm).

TECHNIQUES USED

Darning in loose ends (see page 25)
Joining seams (see page 27)

INSTRUCTIONS
GAUNTLET (WORKED FROM HAND TO ELBOW)

Using 4mm needles, cast on 40 sts.
Row 1: (K1, p1) rep to end of row.
This row forms the 1 x 1 rib patt.
Work 3 more rows in 1 x 1 rib.
Row 5: (K2, p2) rep to end of row.
This row forms the 2 x 2 rib patt.
Rep this row until work meas 13in (33cm) from cast-on edge.
Cast off loosely in 2 x 2 rib.

FINISHING

1 Darn in loose yarn ends.
2 Fold in half lengthwise and starting from the 1 x 1 rib, begin to sew the seam.
3 Sew approx 1½in (4cm) then fasten off.
4 Leave a 2in (5cm) opening for the thumb, then sew remaining seam.
5 Repeat for second gauntlet.
6 Sew on buttons to decorate if desired.

Tip You don't need to change to the 2 x 2 rib if you prefer the look of the 1 x 1 rib. Just continue working the first row pattern to the length required. Then cast off loosely and follow the finishing instructions.

DECREASING STITCHES

SO FAR, ALL THE PROJECTS HAVE BEEN CONSTRUCTED FROM SQUARES AND RECTANGLE SHAPES ONLY. THIS IS FINE FOR SOME ITEMS, BUT IF YOU REALLY WANT TO FURTHER YOUR KNITTING SKILLS YOU WILL NEED TO LEARN TO ADD SOME SHAPE AND DEFINITION TO YOUR PROJECTS.

In this chapter, I will show you how a simple decrease can shape a hat crown so it moulds beautifully to the shape of your head. As well as hat crowns, decreasing can add a waist to a sweater, bodies and limbs to knitted toys and toes to socks – in fact, the possibilities are endless. The basic technique itself is so simple to master that this is definitely a skill worth adding to your repertoire.

Decreasing is reducing the number of stitches on your needle to make the fabric narrower. There are numerous methods of decreasing, which can be a bit daunting for those new to knitting. Each type of decrease is carefully designed to complement the look of the finished article. There can be single or double decreases or tilting decreases that slant either to the left or right.

For now, I am going to keep things simple and teach you the easiest and most universally used decrease in knitting.

Even if you knit other patterns and come across another type of decrease that you are not confident of working, you can safely substitute this one instead. It may not look quite the same as intended by the pattern but will still result in a successful reduction of the stitches.

Here we are going to learn how to decrease one stitch at a time by using the 'knit two stitches together' method, or k2tog, as it is written in its abbreviated form. This decrease slopes to the right on the right side of the work.

SINGLE DECREASE USING THE K2TOG METHOD

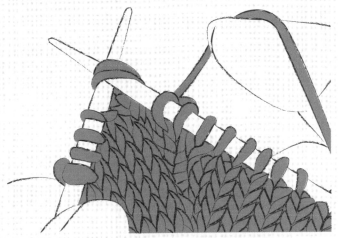

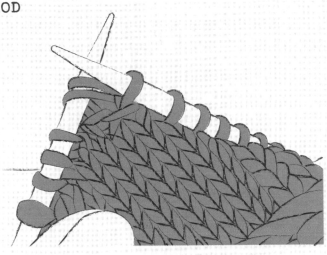

1 Push the tip of the right hand needle through the next two stitches on the left-hand needle from front to back.

2 Knit these stitches together as one.

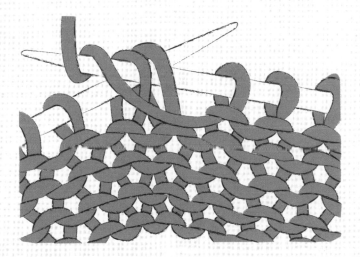

Tip

If you are asked to work a p2tog, simply insert the tip of the right-hand needle into the front of the next 2 stitches and purl them together as one.

BEANIE HAT WITH FELT CORSAGE

A HAT IS MERELY A TUBE WITH SOME SHAPING AT THE TOP OF THE HEAD. WE WILL BEGIN BY KNITTING A RECTANGULAR SHAPE, AS IN PREVIOUS PROJECTS IN THIS BOOK, FOLLOWED BY DECREASES RIGHT NEAR THE END TO SHAPE THE CROWN OF THE HAT.

YOU WILL NEED

Artesano 100% Alpaca DK (109yd/100m per 50g ball)
1 ball in shade Bon Bon
1 pair each 3.25mm (US3:UK10) and 4mm (US6:UK8) needles
Row counter
Tapestry needle
Scissors
3 squares of felt in Black/Mid Grey and Light Grey
Sewing needle and matching sewing thread
Decorative button

TENSION

22 sts and 30 rows to 4in (10cm) over st st using 4mm needles.
Use larger or smaller needles if necessary to obtain correct tension.

FINISHED SIZE

To fit an average-sized woman's head: 20–22in (51–56cm).

TECHNIQUES USED

Knit stitch (see page 36)
Purl stitch (see page 42)
Decreasing (see page 60)
Darning in loose yarn ends (see page 25)
Joining seams (see page 27)

INSTRUCTIONS
HAT (WORKED FROM RIBBED WELT TO CROWN)

Using 3.25mm needles, cast on 104 sts.
Row 1 (RS): (K1, p1) rep to end of row.
Rep this row 5 more times (6 rows in total).
Change to 4mm needles and work in st st as folls:
Row 1 (RS): Knit.
Row 2 (WS): Purl.
Rep these 2 rows until work meas 6in (15cm) from cast-on edge ending on a Row 2.

SHAPE CROWN

Row 1: (K6, k2tog) rep to end of row (91 sts).
Row 2 and all alt rows: Purl.
Row 3: (K5, k2tog) rep to end of row (78 sts).
Row 5: (K4, k2tog) rep to end of row (65 sts).
Row 7: (K3, k2tog) rep to end of row (52 sts).
Row 9: (K2, k2tog) rep to end of row (39 sts).
Row 11: (K1, k2tog) rep to end of row (26 sts).
Row 13: (K2tog) rep to end of row (13 sts).
Row 15: K1, (k2tog) rep to end of row (7 sts).
Break yarn leaving a long tail. Thread the tapestry needle with the yarn end, thread needle through remaining sts on needle, pull them off and pull tight. The top of the hat will gather up and you will see the crown shape form. Fasten off by making a few small stitches. Cut yarn.

FINISHING

1 Darn in loose yarn ends.

2 Fold hat in half lengthwise with right side facing and join rear seam using back stitch.

CORSAGE

1 Cut a strip 9in x 2in (23cm x 5cm) from each of your felt strips.

2 Using your scissors, make vertical cuts downwards along the long edge, each approx ⅛in (3mm) apart. Take each cut nearly down to the opposite edge of your felt but do not cut through it. You should have three strips of fringe.

3 On a flat surface, make a felt sandwich with black on the bottom, mid-grey in the middle and light grey on top. Match the uncut edges to each other.

4 From the short edge, roll up the felt strips into a tight sausage.

5 Thread a sewing needle and contrasting thread and stitch the uncut rolled-up edge very firmly. Keep passing your needle through this base until all the layers are firm and secure. Fasten off.

6 Open out the fringed edges to form a flower. Flatten slightly and position on the hat to one side of the centre just above the ribbed welt. Stitch firmly in place around the corsage base.

7 Sew the button to the centre of the corsage.

INCREASING STITCHES

WE TOUCHED ON SHAPING IN THE PREVIOUS CHAPTER AND LEARNT HOW TO NARROW A PIECE OF RECTANGULAR OR SQUARE KNITTING BY DECREASING. TO COMPLETE OUR SHAPING REPERTOIRE, WE NEED TO LEARN HOW TO WIDEN OUR KNITTING BY INCREASING THE NUMBER OF STITCHES ON THE NEEDLE.

There are myriad ways to make an increase in stitch numbers, some invisible, some leaving a hole and some tilting to the right or left. As you progress with your knitting journey and your confidence grows, you may move onto more complex methods of increasing. But for now, we are going to learn how to increase using the bar technique; this won't show on the right side of your work except for a tiny bar.

The bar increase, shown as kfb in its abbreviated form, is one of the commonest increases. The bar viewed on the right side of the work is simply where the extra stitch was made. This little bar or bump is in fact a wonderful visual aid when you have lost count of the number of increases you have made. Simply count the bars, and you're back on track!

Also, if you want to make an invisible increase while working garter stitch or ribbing, this handy little bar will blend into its surroundings with ease.

THE BAR INCREASE

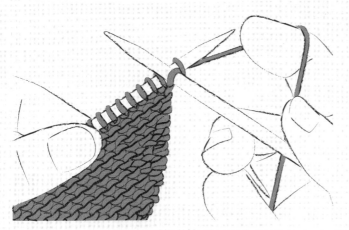

1. Knit into the next stitch on the needle as usual but do not pull it off the left-hand needle.

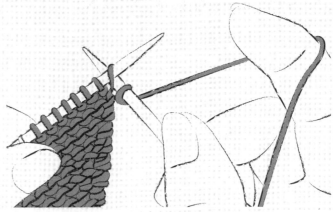

2. Knit into the back loop of the same stitch, inserting your needle from front to back. You may have to stretch the stitch a little to get the needle in.

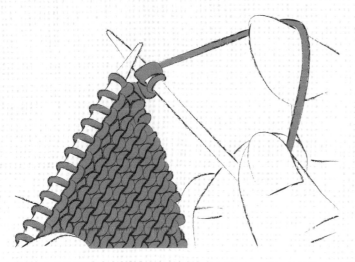

3. Knit this stitch as usual. You now have an extra stitch on your right-hand needle.

Tip If you are asked to increase using pfb, use exactly the same approach. Purl into the front and then the back of the same stitch. It may be a bit tricky as you will need to stretch out the stitch a little but with some practice you will manage to work it.

ENVELOPE CLUTCH BAG

CREATE A BIT OF RETRO CHARM AND SOPHISTICATION WITH THIS QUIRKY LITTLE CLUTCH BAG. YOU COULD ALSO TRY RINGING THE CHANGES BY WHIPPING IT UP IN HOT PINK OR ELECTRIC BLUE AND ADDING A CLASHING BUTTON FOR A STATEMENT COLOUR-POP.

YOU WILL NEED

Manos Del Uruguay Silk Blend 70% extra fine merino, 30% silk (300yd/270m per 100g hank)
1 hank in 2458 Indian
1 pair 4mm (US6:UK8) needles
Tapestry needle
Scissors
¼yd/m of lining material
¼yd/m of interfacing
Sewing needle and thread
Snap fastener
Self-cover button

TENSION

22 sts and 40 rows to 4in (10cm) over garter st using 4mm needles.
Use larger or smaller needles if necessary to obtain correct tension.

TECHNIQUES USED

Knit stitch (see page 36)
Increasing (see page 66)
Darning in loose ends (see page 25)
Joining seams (see page 27)

FINISHED SIZE

9in x 6in (23cm x 15cm)

INSTRUCTIONS

BAG

Using 4mm needles, cast on 3 sts.
Row 1: Knit.
Row 2 (WS): Kfb, k1, kfb (5 sts).
Row 3 and all alt rows: Knit.
Row 4: Kfb, k3, kfb (7 sts).
Row 6: Kfb, k5, kfb (9 sts).
Row 8: Kfb, k7, kfb (11 sts).
Row 10: Kfb, k9, kfb (13 sts).
Cont as set, increasing on the first and last st of every row until you have 49 sts. Now cont to work in garter st (i.e. knit every row) for a further 13in (33cm). Cast off.

FINISHING

1 Darn in loose yarn ends.
2 Lay your knitted piece onto the lining and cut around it, adding a ½in (1cm) seam allowance on all edges.
3 Do the same for the interfacing.

4 Fold the straight cast-off edge of your bag upwards to make an envelope shape. Sew the side seams using mattress stitch (see page 27).

LINING

5 Lay the interfacing on top of the WS of lining. Press the ½in (1cm) seam allowance to WS of pieces along the triangular-shaped edges.
6 With RS facing, fold up the straight bottom edges of the lining pieces to make the same envelope shape as your knitted piece. Sew the side edges.

ASSEMBLY

7 Place the lining in your knitted bag. Using a sewing needle and thread, stitch in place around bag mouth and the inside edge of the triangular flap.
8 Stitch a snap fastener to the inside edge of the flap and to the corresponding piece of bag front. Then cover a self-cover button with a piece of the lining fabric and stitch in place to front of flap.

CABLING

CABLING IS ONE OF THOSE KNITTING TECHNIQUES THAT LOOKS TERRIBLY COMPLICATED AND ADVANCED TO WORK BUT IS EASY WHEN YOU KNOW HOW. ALL YOU NEED, APART FROM YOUR YARN AND NEEDLES, IS ONE LITTLE ACCESSORY: THE CABLE NEEDLE.

Cabling is a method of knitting the row in the usual way but knitting some of the stitches in a different order. In this way, you twist them around each other to form the cable shape.

Sounds complicated? Well, let me take you through the basic cable instructions and I'll bet you'll be whipping up the easy cable placemats and coasters in no time.

All you need to do is work your way through the pattern until you come to the cable instructions, which in this case are either C4B (which means cable 4 stitches to the back of the work) or C4F (which means cable 4 stitches to the front). Then follow the step-by-step instructions, using the photo guides to help, and hey presto – you are cabling!

Tip Choose the correct cable needle for the yarn you are using. If the yarn is very chunky, you will need to use a thick cable needle. Likewise, if the yarn is lightweight, you will need a finer cable needle.

CABLE NEEDLES

A cable needle is a small version of a double-pointed knitting needle, sometimes with a kink in the middle. The kink is for safely holding stitches you are not using. It makes it easy to slip them back onto the working needle when the pattern tells you, so you can knit them as usual.

C4B (CABLE 4 TO THE BACK)

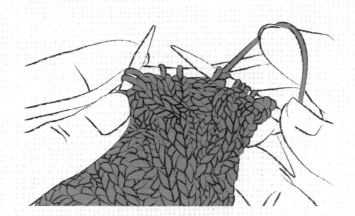

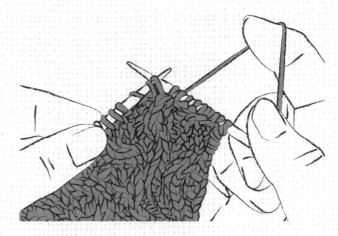

1 Slip the next 2 sts from the left-hand needle onto the cable needle and move the cable needle to the back of the work.

2 Knit the next 2 sts from the left-hand needle as usual, then move the cable needle to the front of the work. Now knit the 2 stitches from the cable needle.

C4F (CABLE 4 TO THE FRONT)

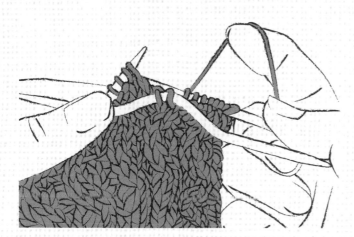

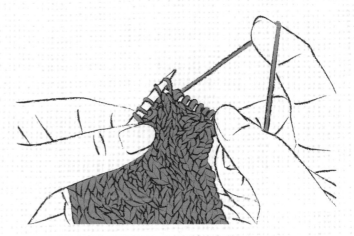

1 Slip the next 2 sts from the left-hand needle onto the cable needle and hold the cable needle at the front of the work.

2 Knit the next 2 sts from the left-hand needle, as usual. Now knit the 2 sts from cable needle.

CABLED PLACEMATS AND COASTERS

ALWAYS THOUGHT CABLES WERE DIFFICULT? FEAR NOT: WITH MY SIMPLE GUIDE YOU WILL BE ABLE TO CREATE THIS CHIC TABLE SET WITHOUT TEARS. IMPRESS ALL YOUR FRIENDS WITH YOUR NEW-FOUND KNITTING SKILLS WHEN YOU THROW A DINNER PARTY JUST TO SHOW THEM OFF.

YOU WILL NEED

Blacker Yarns Pure Galway Wool Aran (76yd/70m per 50g ball)
One placemat: 2 balls
Two coasters: 1 ball
1 pair 5mm (US8:UK6) needles
Chunky cable needle
Row counter

TENSION

22 sts and 48 rows to 4in (10cm) over cable patt using 5mm needles.
Use larger or smaller needles if necessary to obtain correct tension.

TECHNIQUES USED

Knit stitch (see page 36)
Purl stitch (see page 42)
Cabling (see page 70)
Darning in loose ends (see page 25)
Joining seams (see page 27)
Pinning and blocking (see page 26)

FINISHED SIZE

Placemat: 10½in x 14½in (27cm x 37cm)
Coaster: 4in x 4½in (10cm x 11cm)

SPECIAL ABBREVIATIONS

C4B (cable four back): slip next 2 stitches onto a cable needle and hold at back of work, knit 2 stitches, then knit 2 stitches from cable needle
C4F (cable four front): slip next 2 stitches onto a cable needle and hold at front of work, knit 2 stitches, then knit 2 stitches from cable needle

INSTRUCTIONS

PLACEMAT

Using 5mm needles, cast on 66 sts.
Knit 2 rows.
Row 1 (RS): K2, (p2, k4) rep to last 4 sts, p2, k2.
Row 2 (WS): K2, (k2, p4) rep to last 4 sts, k4.
Row 3: K2, (p2, C4B) rep to last 4 sts, p2, k2.
Row 4: As Row 2.
Rows 5 and 6: As Rows 1 and 2.
Row 7: K2, (p2, C4F) rep to last 4 sts, p2, k2.
Row 8: As Row 2.
These 8 rows set the pattern.
Rep these 8 rows until work meas 14½in (37cm) ending on a Row 4.
Knit 2 rows.
Cast off.

COASTER

Using 5mm needles, cast on 24 sts.
Knit 2 rows.
Work 8 rows in pattern as for placemat.
Knit 2 rows.
Cast off.

FINISHING

1 Darn in loose yarn ends on all pieces.
2 Pin and block each piece and press into shape with a steam iron (see page 26).
3 Don't be afraid to flatten out the cables slightly, using the steam button.

LACE KNITTING

LACE IS A BROAD DESCRIPTION OF AN OPENWORK STYLE OF KNITTING – A COMBINATION OF HOLES AND EYELETS WORKED OVER A BACKGROUND OF KNITTED FABRIC. IT CAN TRANSFORM AN OTHERWISE PLAIN PIECE OF KNITTING INTO SOMETHING MUCH MORE INTERESTING AND TACTILE.

Lace techniques can be used to create anything from the frilly and ornate to plain and geometric, right through to a chunkier, rustic piece with large Swiss-cheese holes (think Vivienne Westwood's mesh punk sweaters). Even if you think you are not a 'lacy' sort of person, I can guarantee there will be one form of lace stitch that is right for you.

It's not true that lace knitting is too complex for a beginner. Just follow my step-by-step guide and with a little concentration and perseverance, you will be able to master this technique.

In its simplest form, lace knitting is simply a series of holes (or eyelets) created by working a 'yarn over'. This means you wrap the yarn around your needle wherever you want your hole to appear within the lace. If you want a normal hole, you wrap the yarn around the needle once and if you want a larger hole, wrap the yarn around twice or even three times. By creating this hole using 'yarn over', you will have added one, two or even three more stitches to your row. Now you need to decrease the same number of stitches

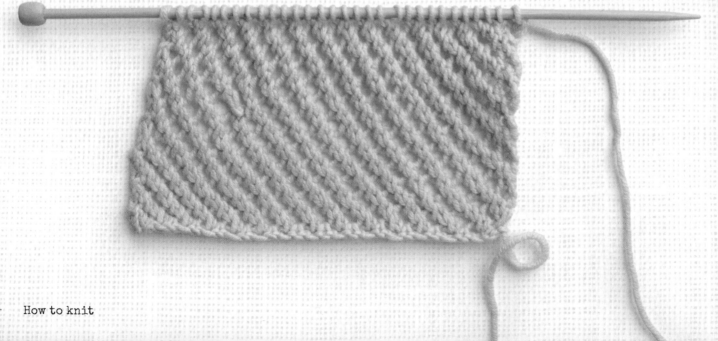

to maintain the same number of stitches you started with. This is why all lace-stitch patterns follow a sequence: make a hole (yo) and then make a decrease (k2tog).

Most lace patterns are smooth-surfaced, having a stocking-stitch base with the wrong sides purled. Some have a garter-stitch base, which makes them heavier but also reversible. The really

open-net type laces have yarn overs worked on every row. Even seasoned knitters need a degree of concentration to knit this type of lace successfully. But although lace knitting can take more time and perseverance than the average stocking-stitch project, the results are definitely worthwhile.

Tip With lace, it is best to only count your row stitches at the end of each repeat. This is because the yarn overs and decreases may add or decrease the original number of stitches on some of the interim rows. However, you will always end up with the correct amount after the last row of every repeat.

BLOCK YOUR WORK

You may find your finished lace doesn't look like the picture in your pattern. You have probably done nothing wrong, but you need to open out the eyelets and 'set' the pattern. To do this, you should block your work on a blocking board.

Place the piece on the blocking board and steam it with a steam iron. While it is still damp, stretch it out with your fingers so it takes on the shape you want. Use pins to hold it in place on the blocking board and leave to dry completely. When you remove it, the lace work will stay open and pretty.

READING AND WORKING THE LACE PATTERN

First, familiarize yourself with the pattern repeat. Don't risk going straight into the project; instead, work a swatch to see how the lace pattern works over a row. Look at row 1 of your lace pattern. Here you will find a set of instructions (yarn overs and decreases with perhaps some knitted stitches in between) that you will generally be asked to repeat a set number of times across the row. Check all the abbreviations on page 33 and make sure you know how to work all the stitches mentioned before you start.

YO (YARN OVER)

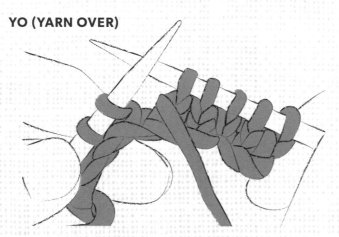

1 Knit the number of stitches stated in the pattern row, then bring your yarn to the front of the work between the points of your needles.

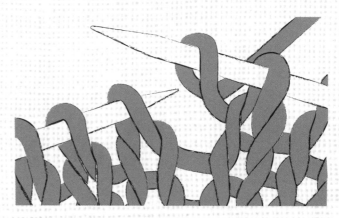

2 With the yarn in front, wrap it over the top of the right-hand needle from front to back. Work the next stitch as noted in the pattern row.

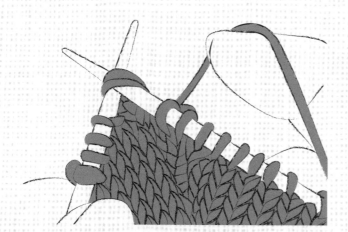

K2TOG (KNIT 2 STITCHES TOGETHER)

Push the tip of the right-hand needle through the next two stitches on the left-hand needle from front to back. Knit these stitches together as one.

TRICKS TO HELP WHEN YOU KNIT LACE

MARK YOUR REPEAT

Work your first repeat, place a stitch marker (see page 16), work your second repeat, place a stitch marker then continue to place a stitch marker after every repeat across the row. Check the stitches are the same across every repeat before you move on to row 2.

PUT IN A 'LIFELINE'

When you have worked all the rows of the first lace pattern sequence, add a lifeline before beginning the next set of the stitch pattern. Simply thread a length of contrasting thread through a needle, then through all the stitches on the row. Begin knitting again. If you make a mistake in your knitting and cannot repair it, slip everything off the needle and go back to your lifeline. Place the stitches back onto your needle and start again at row 1 of the pattern.

CHUNKY LACE COWL

THIS CHUNKY LACE COWL IS THE PERFECT INTRODUCTION TO LACE KNITTING. USING LARGE NEEDLES AND THICK YARN, YOU'LL KNIT UP THIS COSY PROJECT IN NO TIME. FINISH IT WITH YOUR CHOICE OF DECORATIVE BUTTONS TO CREATE A CLASSIC WINTER WARMER.

YOU WILL NEED

Blue Sky Alpacas 100% organic cotton (150yd/137m per 100g hank)
2 hanks 80 Bone
1 pair 6mm (US10:UK4) needles
4 wooden buttons
Sewing needle and matching thread

TENSION

16 sts and 16 rows to 4in (10cm) over simple lace patt using 6mm needles. Tension not critical.

FINISHED SIZE

10in x 28in (25cm x 71cm)

TECHNIQUES USED

Knit stitch (see page 36)
Purl stitch (see page 42)
Lace: yarn over and knitting two stitches together (see page 74)
Darning in loose yarn ends (see page 25)

INSTRUCTIONS

COWL

Using 6mm needles, cast on 40 sts.
Knit 2 rows.
Begin working in simple lace patt as folls:
Row 1 (RS): K2, (yo, k2tog) rep to last 2 sts, k2.
Row 2 (WS): K2, p to last 2 sts, k2.
Row 3: K4, (yo, k2tog) rep to last 4 sts, k2tog, k2.
Row 4: As Row 2.
Rep these 4 rows until cowl meas 28in (71cm) ending on a Row 4.
Knit 2 rows.
Cast off.

FINISHING

1 Darn in loose yarn ends.
2 Sew the four buttons along one short edge of the cowl along the garter stitch hem. Place one at each corner and space the remaining buttons evenly in between.
3 Use eyelets to fasten.

Tip Use a row counter to keep track of which row you are on in the pattern repeat.

BUTTONHOLES

AS WELL AS CARDIGANS AND COATS, BUTTONHOLES CAN ALSO BE USED TO CLOSE A VARIETY OF OTHER KNITTED PROJECTS AND ACCESSORIES FROM PURSES AND CUSHION COVERS TO PHONE COVERS, SO IT IS DEFINITELY WORTHWHILE MASTERING THIS TECHNIQUE EVEN IF YOU DON'T PLAN ON KNITTING LARGE GARMENTS YET.

I have bad and good news about learning how to work buttonholes. Firstly, there are several ways to make them. Once you have learnt how to master one technique, you will come across a pattern working the buttonhole in a completely different manner. But don't let that put you off. I will show you a version that is commonly used.

The good news is that a buttonhole is merely a decorative hole. If you have already worked through the lace technique on pages 74–77, you already know how to make a buttonhole! The principle is the same: the hole is made by wrapping your yarn around the needle to make a stitch (yarn over) then, because you have now made an extra stitch, decreasing a stitch by knitting the next two stitches together. The pattern instructions will tell you exactly where and how many times to make your buttonhole. All you have to do is work your way through the row and when you come to the buttonhole instructions – yo, k2tog – follow the information given here.

WORKING A YARN-OVER BUTTONHOLE

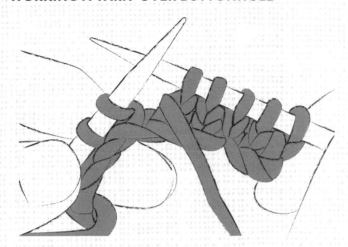

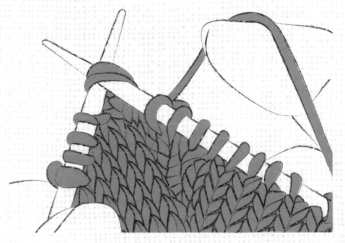

1 Knit the number of stitches stated in the pattern row, then bring your yarn to the front of the work between the points of your needles (see page 76). With the yarn in front, wrap it over the top of the right-hand needle from front to back.

2 Push the tip of the right-hand needle through the next two stitches on the left-hand needle from front to back. Knit these stitches together as one.

ALTERNATIVE METHOD

An alternative instruction for making a buttonhole is made across two rows. On the first row (usually the right side), you cast off two or three stitches. On the second row, you cast on either two or three stitches opposite each of the cast-off stitches. This method can form a larger buttonhole, so is good when you want to use an especially large button that might not fit through the regular 'yarn over' type buttonhole.

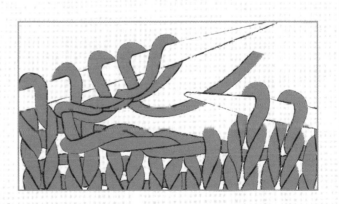

PATCHWORK CUSHION COVER

EACH PATCHWORK SQUARE IN THIS CUSHION USES DIFFERENT COMBINATIONS OF THE KNIT AND PURL STITCH TO CREATE FOUR INDIVIDUAL TEXTURES AND STITCH PATTERNS. THE CUSHION COVER IS CONSTRUCTED IN A SIMPLE ENVELOPE STYLE WITH BUTTON FASTENINGS SO YOU CAN PRACTISE YOUR BUTTONHOLE-MAKING SKILLS.

YOU WILL NEED

King Cole Merino Blend Chunky 100% wool (73yd/67m per 50g ball)
6 balls in shade 909 Pebble
1 pair 6mm (US10:UK4) needles
Tapestry needle
Sewing needle and matching sewing thread
7 assorted buttons
16in (41cm) cushion pad

TENSION

Square one: double moss stitch
19 sts and 24 rows to 4in (10cm) using 6mm needles.
Square two: lizard lattice stitch
14 sts and 20 rows to 4in (10cm) using 6mm needles.
Square three: diagonal seed stitch
18 sts and 22 rows to 4in (10cm) using 6mm needles.
Square four: tile stitch
18 sts and 22 rows to 4in (10cm) using 6mm needles.
Use larger or smaller needles if necessary to obtain correct tension.

FINISHED SIZE

Each square measures 8in x 8in (20cm x 20cm)
To fit a 16in (41cm) cushion pad

TECHNIQUES USED

Knit stitch (see page 36)
Purl stitch (see page 42)
Working a buttonhole (see page 80)
Darning in loose yarn ends (see page 25)
Joining seams (see page 27)

Tip The beauty of this sampler cushion is that you can use any variety of interesting stitch patterns. Just choose a pattern you'd like to master (there are books of stitch patterns available to buy or many free samples on the Internet if you search for them), work a tension swatch first and then calculate how many stitches you would need to cast on to make 8in (20cm). Work the new pattern until your square measures 8in (20cm) long, then cast off.

INSTRUCTIONS

SQUARE ONE:
DOUBLE MOSS STITCH

Using 6mm needles, cast on 39 sts.

Row 1 (RS): K1, (p1, k1) rep to end of row.

Row 2 (WS): P1, (k1, p1) rep to end of row.

Row 3: As Row 2.

Row 4: As Row 1.

These 4 rows form double moss stitch.

Rep these 4 rows until square meas 8in (20cm)

Cast off in patt.

SQUARE TWO:
LIZARD LATTICE STITCH

Using 6mm needles, cast on 27 sts.

Row 1 (RS): Knit.

Row 2 (WS): Purl.

These 2 rows form st st.

Rep last 2 rows once more.

Row 5 (RS): P3, (k3, p3) rep to end.

Row 6: Purl.

Rep last 2 rows once more then Row 5 again.

Starting with a p row, work 5 rows in st st.

Row 15: K3, (p3, k3) rep brackets to end.

Row 16: Purl.

Rep last 2 rows once more then Row 15 again.

Starting with a p row, work 5 rows in st st.

Beg from Row 5, rep lizard lattice patt once more.

Cast off in patt.

SQUARE THREE:
DIAGONAL SEED STITCH

Using 6mm needles, cast on 36 sts.

Row 1 (RS): (K5, p1) to end.

Row 2 (WS): P1, (k1, p5) to last 5 sts, k1, p4.

Row 3: K3, (p1, k5) to last 3 sts, p1, k2.

Row 4: P3, (k1, p5) to last 3 sts, k1, p2.

Row 5: K1, (p1, k5) rep to last 5 sts, p1, k4.

Row 6: (P5, k1) to end.

Rep these 6 rows until square meas 8in (20cm) ending on a WS row.

Cast off in patt.

SQUARE FOUR:
TILE STITCH

Using 6mm needles cast on 34 sts.

Row 1 (RS): K4, (p2, k4) rep to end.

Row 2 (WS): p4, (k2, p4) rep to end.

Rep last 2 rows twice more.

Row 7: As Row 2.

Row 8: As Row 1.

Rep these 8 rows until square meas 8in (20cm) ending on a WS row

Cast off in pattern.

BACK FLAP WITH
BUTTON BAND

Using 6mm needles, cast on 56 sts.

Row 1 (RS): Knit.

Row 2 (WS): Purl.

These 2 rows form st st.

Cont in st st until work meas 8in (20cm) ending on a p row. **

Button band

Work in k2 x p2 rib as folls:

Row 1: (K2, p2) rep to end of row.

Rep this row 8 times.

Cast off in patt.

BACK FLAP WITH
BUTTONHOLE BAND

Work as for back flap up to **

Buttonhole band

Work 2 rows in k2 x p2 rib as for back flap.

Row 3 (Buttonhole): Patt 6, yo, k2tog, (k5, yo, k2tog) rep brackets 6 times, patt rem 6 sts.

Work 5 rows in k2 x p2 rib.

Cast off in patt.

FINISHING

1 Darn in loose yarn ends.

2 Sew the four patchwork squares together using mattress stitch, making sure the edges line up accurately.

3 With RS tog, position the back pieces on top of the front piece.

4 Make sure the ribbed edges overlap at the centre part of the cushion.

5 Pin and stitch around all four sides.

6 Turn RS out. Sew the 7 buttons evenly along the button band to correspond with each buttonhole.

Yarn Suppliers

UK

Artesano Ltd
Unit G, Lambs Farm Business Park
Basingstoke Road
Swallowfield
Reading
Berkshire
RG7 1PQ
Tel: +44 (0)118 9503350
Internet stockist: www.angelyarns.co.uk
www.artesanoyarns.co.uk

Blacker Designs
Unit B, Pipers Court
Pennygillam Way
Launceston
Cornwall
PL15 7PJ
Tel: +44 (0)1566 777635
www.blackerdesigns.co.uk

King Cole Ltd
Merrie Mills
Snaygill Industrial Estate
Keighley Road
Skipton
North Yorkshire
BD23 2QR
Tel: +44 (0)1756 703670
www.kingcole.co.uk

Manos Del Uruguay
Unit G, Lambs Farm Business Park
Basingstoke Road
Swallowfield
Reading
Berkshire
RG7 1PQ
Tel: +44 (0)118 9503350
www.artesanoyarns.co.uk

The Natural Fibre Company/
Blacker Designs
Unit B, Pipers Court
Pennygilliam Way
Launceston
Cornwall
PL15 7PJ
Tel: +44 (0)1566 777635
www.blackerdesigns.co.uk

US

Blue Sky Alpacas Inc.
PO Box 88
Cedar
MN 55011
Tel: 763-753-5815/888-460-8862
www.blueskyalpacas.com

Brown Sheep Yarn Company
10 0662 County Road 16
Mitchell
NE 69357
Tel: 800-826-9136
www.brownsheep.com

Cascade Yarns
1224 Andover Park E
Tukwila
WA 98188
Tel: 206-574-0440
www.cascadeyarns.com

Useful Websites

www.knittinghelp.com

This website offers free knitting videos for beginners, a knitters' forum plus free patterns too. A wonderful resource for all beginners to the craft.

www.learn2knit.co.uk

A site with comprehensive instructions and illustrations for all the knitting basics.

www.purlbee.com/beginners-knits/

The home of Purl Sohos craft blog. It's a great site with super photo guides plus tons of really gorgeous free patterns.

www.ravelry.com

A fantastic site where you can meet with other knitters to ask questions about knitting, join online groups for your particular knitting passion (i.e., lace knitting/beginner knits/knitted dinosaurs, etc.), browse the huge battalion of pattern downloads (many of them free) and find out what's going on in your area.

www.ukhandknitting.com

The website of the UK Handknitting Association. A fabulous mine of information for new knitters plus free patterns and loads of charity knits, too.

www.yarnaddict.co.uk

The website of lace-knitting designer Anniken Allis. As well as selling her patterns, Anniken also has an online knitting school where she teaches a variety of knitting techniques including knitting Continental style.

www.youtube.com

A great site with hundreds of videos showing all the knitting basics. Just type in what you'd like to view, such as casting on, and you will find dozens of keen knitters who have uploaded videos sharing their knowledge and skills just for you.

About the Author

Tina Barrett was taught to knit by her grandmother and has been passionate about creating her own gorgeous yarn and fabric-based designs ever since. She is a regular contributor to many knitting and sewing magazines and is the author of five previous books for GMC Publications: *Knits for Dogs and Cats*, *Natural Knits for Babies and Toddlers*, *Natural Crochet for Babies and Toddlers*, *Home Sewn Nursery* and *Knitted Dinosaurs*. Tina lives with her family in Cornwall, south-west England.

Acknowledgements

Thanks must go to the chaps at GMC: Managing Editor Gerrie Purcell, Senior Project Editor Dominique Page for her excellent editorial skills and Rob Janes who made such a wonderful job of the design. Thanks also to Rachel Vowles for her pattern-checking ability, Peters & Zabransky for the artwork and Sarah Cuttle and Rebecca Mothersole who took such beautiful photographs.

Special thanks go to all those who shared enthusiasm for the project and donated yarn and notions. I hope I have done you all proud: Tom and Jenny Comber of Artesano, Sue Blacker and all the guys at The Natural Fibre Company, Lance Martin at King Cole Blue Sky Alpacas.

A huge thanks to my mum's 'model hands' and patience during the taking of all the step-by-step reference photographs and to 'David Bailey' (long-suffering hubby) who took the said shots.

Also to my mum again, for her knitting skills and helping with some of the projects in this book.

To my ever-patient husband and children, who still glaze over when it comes to woolly things – poor misguided souls. You are yet to see the light.

And finally, to my grandmother, Emily, who sadly passed away when I was just twenty; after you'd patiently collected up my knitting when I'd hurled it across the room in frustration and quietly picked up the dropped stitches yet again, did you ever dream it would come to this?

Index

To order a book, or to request
a catalogue, contact:

GMC Publications Ltd
Castle Place, 166 High Street,
Lewes, East Sussex,
BN7 1XU
United Kingdom
Tel: +44 (0)1273 488005
www.gmcbooks.com